celtic cookbook

156 traditional recipes from the 6 Celtic nations

Collected by HELEN SMITH-TWIDDY

Y Lolfa

Argraffiad cyntaf: Chwefror 1979 *(1st impression: February 1979)*
Ail argraffiad: Medi 1979 *(2nd impression: September 1979)*

© Y Lolfa 1979

ISBN: 0 904864 50 2

Y Lolfa

Argraffwyd a chyhoeddwyd yng Nghymru
gan Y Lolfa, Talybont, Ceredigion SY24 5ER; ffôn (097086) 304.
Printed & published in Wales by Y Lolfa at above address.

Contents

Conversion Tables

FLUID & DRY WEIGHTS

American	British
16 fluid ozs.	20 fluid ozs.
½ American pint	8 fluid ozs.
1 cup American	8 oz. cup
1 tablespoon	1 dessertspoon
1¼ pints	1 pint
½ cup	8 dessertspoon
1 cup sugar	7 ozs.
1 cup flour	4 ozs.
1 cup butter	7 ozs.
1 cup fruit	6 ozs.

METRIC CONVERSION

1 oz.	28.3 grms.
2 oz.	56.6 grms.
4 oz.	113.3 grms.
8 oz.	226.7 grms.
1 lb.	453.3 grms.
1 fl. oz.	28.4 millilitres
1 pint	568 millilitres
1 level cup	250 ml.
¼ level cup	125 ml.
1 tablespoon	20 ml.
1 teaspoon	5 ml.
1 gram	0.0353 ozs.
1 kilogram	2.20 lbs.
1 millilitre	0.0352 fl. ozs.
1 litre	1.76 pints

HEAT Conversion Table

Gas		Electricity
¼	Cool	225°F
½	Cool	250
1	Very Slow	275
2	Slow	300
3	Slow	325
4	Moderate	350
5	Moderate	375
6	Hot	400
7	Hot	425
8	Very Hot	450
9	Very Hot	475

soups

Consomme

1 quart of good beef stock
½ lb. stewing beef
3 tablespoons sweet sherry
Seasonings
Vegetables : selection of carrots, onions, cauliflower and turnip

Make sure there is no fat on the stock. Cut up meat and vegetables into small pieces. Place in a large saucepan. Season. Cook until the meat is tender. Strain through a clean cloth or sieve. Add the sherry just before serving. Sprinkle some chopped parsley on top prior to serving.

Bouilleabaise

2 lbs. assorted fish (e.g. halibut, salmon, shrimp, sole, trout)
1 lb. fish trimmings (heads, tails etc.)
4 pts cold water
3 fresh peeled tomatoes
teaspoon orange juice
6 whole peppercorns
salt to taste
cup grated Swiss cheese

1 lb. boiled new potatoes
small onion
2 leeks (white part only)
2 good pinches of chopped parsley
1 clove garlic – minced
pinch of thyme and sage
very small pinch of saffron

Make the stock from the fish trimmings and water. Strain and leave to get cold. Chop up vegetables, but not the potatoes – and cook on low heat until soft and golden in colour. Add the sage, thyme and saffron. Add tomatoes, stock, salt and peppercorns. Add next the fish, the thickest pieces on the bottom of the saucepan and the shrimps on the top. Cover and cook for about five minutes fairly rapidly, then reduce heat and cook until the fish pieces flake easily when turned on a fork. Five minutes before serving add the Swiss cheese and more salt if needed. Serve on large shallow platters with long crusty bread.

St. Brieuc Vegetable Soup

4 quarts of meat stock
4 large peeled tomatoes
2 lbs green beans
6 large potatoes

seasonings
½ cup pasta sheets
3 cups grated Swiss cheese

In a very large pan place the stock and seasonings. Bring to the boil slowly. Chop up the tomatoes : clean and string beans. Peel potatoes and cut up into small pieces. Break pasta sheets into manageable pieces. Add the vegetables and pasta to the stock and cook slowly until vegetables are cooked. Before serving add half the cheese — do not boil once the cheese has been added. Put remainder of cheese in a bowl and serve with the soup at the table.

Pot au Feu

1 quart cold water
1 lb. stewing beef (preferably shin)
1 each leek, carrot, turnip, swede, stick of celery, cabbage, large potato.
2 oz. rice
Bouquet garni
a pinch of nutmeg
a few cloves
a pinch of peppercorn

Tie the meat to keep its shape. Place in a large stewpot with the water. Simmer slowly for an hour. Peel, wash and cut up the vegetables into small pieces. Add to the meat. Add seasonings and cook for another hour. About ¼ hour before the end of the cooking time, add the rice. Serve very hot with fresh crusty bread.

If this soup is not all finished at one serving, more vegetables can be added as needed and cooked again. A Pot au Feu is always cooking in most kitchens in France.

Onion Soup

2 lbs. onions
2 quarts good beef stock
1 cup grated Swiss cheese
¾ cup strong Parmesan cheese
½ cup port or sherry
3 oz. butter
1 oz. flour
Seasonings

Cut onions into rings. Melt butter in a large pan and add onions. Cook until transparent. Sprinkle the flour over the onions and allow the flour to be absorbed. Add the seasonings. Cook slowly until the onions are tender. Add the Parmesan cheese and cook another 15 minutes or so. Before serving add port or sherry and bring back to the boil. Add the Swiss cheese and serve with croutons.

Chowder

4 rashers bacon (chopped)
2 pints white sauce
1 cup diced carrots
1 lb. fresh peas (cooked)
2 oz. butter
2 small onions (chopped)
2 cups diced potatoes
1 cup chopped celery
1 lb. cooked shell fish
seasonings

Heat the butter in a large pan. Fry the onions and bacon lightly. Add the chopped and diced vegetables. Add the white sauce and seasonings. Add the fish. Simmer for about 15 minutes. Serve with Dorset Knobs. (Recipe in Bread section.)

Shrimp Soup

1¼ cup cooked prawns
1 pint water
salt and pepper
1 oz. butter
1½ pints fresh milk
1 pint potato soup
dash of paprika
2 small chopped onions

Melt butter in a large pan. Add fish and cook slightly (until warmed through). Add the other ingredients. Season. Bring just to the boil but do *not* boil. Keep just at simmering point for 10 minutes. Chill and serve with chopped onions and parsley on the top. Dust with paprika.

Potato Soup

3 lbs. old potatoes
6 pints good brown stock
½ lb. butter
½ pint thin cream or top of the milk

½ doz. large leeks
seasonings

Melt the butter in a large stew pot. Add the chopped up potatoes and the leeks (chopped up into small pieces). Cook until tender. Season. Add the stock and cook for 2 hours. Before serving add the cream.

Ham and Pea Soup

1 lb. piece of boiling ham
½ lb. diced peas
pinch of parsley
1 oz. flour
4 medium onions
Seasonings
4 oz. butter
4 large potatoes
2½ pints white stock

Wash and cut up the vegetables. Melt butter. Add
the vegetables and the meat chopped up into small
pieces. Brown slightly. Season. Add the soaked peas
and stock. Simmer for 2 hours, on a low heat.
Thicken with the flour if necessary before serving.

Fish Soup

2 lbs. assorted shell fish (cockles, clams, mussels and
some white fish)
2 small potatoes
3 pints of fish stock
Cream, about 3 tablespoons
2 small onions
seasonings
pinch of parsley

Remove the fish from the shells. Add the diced
potatoes and onions to the shell fish and season.
Pour the stock over. Simmer until the vegetables
and fish are cooked and before serving add the cream.
Sprinkle parsley over the top. Do not boil once the
cream has been added as the soup will curdle.

ISLE OF MAN

Manx Broth

1 lb. shin of beef
1 lb. mixed chopped vegetables (potatoes, carrots,
turnip and onions)
1 oz. parsley
salt and black pepper
2 -3 oz. barley

Place the piece of meat into a large soup pan and
cover with cold water. Simmer gently until the meat
is cooked. Take out and put on a platter. (This can
be used cold for another meal). Add the diced
vegetables and season. Simmer gently for 1 hour.
Ten minutes before serving this soup drop in small
parsley dumplings and cook in the broth. Make as
follows :

4 oz. plain flour
1 oz. butter
1 oz. parsley
few drops water

Rub butter into flour. Add parsley. Make into a soft dough. Form into small balls.

This is a dish that is still served on the Island when the wedding feast is a sit down one.

SCOTTISH

Cock a Leekie

1 boiling fowl
2 quarts of stock
salt and pepper
1 bunch of leeks
1 lb. onions (white)

Put the fowl in a large pot. Cover with the stock and diced vegetables. Season. Simmer for 3 - 4 hours. Cool. Skim the fat from the top. Re-heat to serve and serve very hot with fresh bread.

1 sheep's head
1 mutton flank
½ cup barley
½ cup dried peas
salt and pepper·
approx 2 quarts water

Clean the head and place in water overnight. Clean out the eyes and remove the brain. Place the head and mutton in sufficient water to cover, and simmer for 1 hour. Cool and skim off fat. Peel and slice vegetables and add to the broth. Cook for a further 2 hours. Serve hot.

Powsowdie

6 large carrots
6 large onions
4 small turnips
4 small potatoes
1 leek
parsley

Partan Bree

1 large crab (boiled)
1½ pint white stock
3 oz. rice
¼ pint cream
Drop of anchovy essence
1 pint milk

Take the meat from the crab. Place milk and rice in a saucepan and bring to the boil. Simmer until rice is soft. Season. Add stock, crab meat and essence. Stir until it boils. Stir in cream but do not boil after cream has been added. Serve hot.

Scotch Broth

1 neck of lamb
½ cabbage
4 dried carrots
2 onions

1 leek
1 small turnip
parsley
salt and pepper
4 oz. dried peas
4 small potatoes
4 oz. pearl barley
2 quarts water

Soak the peas overnight, or until soft. Discard the water. Place meat, seasonings, barley and the peas in a large pot. Simmer for 2 - 3 hours. Peel and chop the vegetables and add about one hour before serving. Serve hot.

WALES

Cawl Cennin

3 lbs. best end of neck
1 lb. leeks
2 onions
2 carrots
1 turnip
1 swede
salt and pepper
parsnips
8 potatoes
¼ cabbage

3 tablespoons chopped parsley
10 cups water

Trim the fat from the meat. Peel and cut up the vegetables into small cubes. Cover with the water and add the seasoning. Cook for about 2 hours very slowly. Skim off any fat before serving.

Serve as a main meal with fresh bread.

Traditionally cawl has to be eaten with a wooden spoon from a wooden bowl. This way there is no fear of burning mouth or fingers.

Pembroke Soup

3 doz. shelled and prepared oysters
3 pints good fish stock (made from fish heads etc.)
2 large chopped onions
2 oz. butter
2 oz. flour
salt and pepper
pinch of cinnamon

Simmer gently for about ¾ hour the stock onion and seasonings. Melt the butter and stir in the flour. Thicken the stock with this. Sieve if there are any lumps. Put the oysters into a large soup bowl, pour the boiling soup over and serve with small brown rolls. (Recipe in Bread Section).

Cawl Afu

1 pigs liver
2 pints water
1 lb. onions
salt and pepper
1 lb. potatoes
1 lb. carrots, swede and parsnips (cut into small cubes).

Cut up the liver and onions into small cubes. Gently simmer with the water for 2 hours. Add only the pepper at this stage as the salt toughens the liver. Half an hour before serving add the other vegetables.

Cook gently and serve hot. The liver, after all the cooking, should have become almost like a puree.

This soup was made when the farm pig met his doom. The bladder was blown up and used by the children as a football.

Cawl

2 lbs. best end of neck
2 lbs. potatoes
1 lb. bacon
seasoning
water
1 lb. leeks
1 lb. onions
1 lb. carrots, swede or turnip

Trim meat and brown. Peel and cut vegetables into cubes. Place diced bacon and neck, plus seasoning into a crochan (a large Welsh stewpan) and cover with water. Simmer for 1 hour. Add vegetables and simmer for another hour.

Serve hot with fresh bread.

bread

Savarin

4 cups plain flour
1 cup warm milk
8 eggs
6 tablespoons sugar
½ cup warm water
1 cup sliced almonds
salt
½ lb. melted butter
1½ oz. yeast

Savarin Sauce :
2 cups sugar
1 oz. orange juice
1 oz. lemon juice
2 cups water
¼ cup rum or cointreau

Put all ingredients in a saucepan and bring to the boil. Cool and use as needed.

Mix yeast and water together. Add a very small amount of the sugar. Cream the butter and sugar together. Add the eggs one at a time : add the warm milk and flour. Leave in a warm place to prove until double in size. (This will take about 2 hours.) Knead. Grease a savarin ring and sprinkle almonds on the base. Pour in yeast batter and prove again for about an hour. Bake in hot oven for ½ hour. Cool.

Make holes in the ring by poking with a skewer. Pour the savarin sauce over and serve with cream. This mixture makes two savarin rings of about a dozen servings each.

Brioche

1 oz. yeast
½ cup warm water
1 oz. sugar

Mix together and allow to stand for 5 minutes. When the yeast has activated, add teaspoon salt,

1 teaspoon salt
4 small eggs,
¼ lb. warmed butter
3½ cups plain flour

Mix until dough is smooth. Leave to prove for about 1½ hours until double in size. Knead again and place in refrigerator in a greased container for 24 hours. Next day, shape into small or a large brioche and cook for about 1 hour for the large and about 20 minutes for the petite brioches.

Dorset Knobs

    1 lb. plain flour
    ½ oz. yeast
    1 oz. butter
    pinch of salt
    ½ oz. sugar
    ½ pint warm milk

Cream the sugar and yeast. Add the melted butter to the milk and add to the flour. Knead to a smooth dough. Form into small rolls and leave to prove for one hour in a warm spot. Bake in a hot oven for 20 minutes.

Drop Scones

    ½ lb. self-raising flour
    1 egg (beaten)
    ¼ pint milk
    pinch of salt
    2 oz. butter
    1 oz. sugar

Rub butter into flour. Add other ingredients and mix to a soft dough. Roll on floured board. Cut into rounds. Bake in a hot oven for 12-15 minutes or until golden brown.

Redruth Tea Cake

Overnight soak 1 cup cold tea: 1 lb. dried mixed fruit: 1 cup brown sugar.

Next day add 2 cups self-raising flour: 1 well beaten egg and pinch of salt. Mix well. Pour into greased loaf tin and bake in moderate oven for 1½ hours. Leave one whole day before cutting.

Wholemeal Bread

    2 cups wholemeal flour
    ½ oz. sugar
    1 tablespoon golden syrup
    ½ oz. yeast
    pinch salt
    1½ cup warm milk

Cream the yeast and sugar. Add the syrup and milk. Make a well in the centre of the flour and pour in the liquid. Knead. Let prove for about an hour in a warm place. Punch down and form into round loaves. Leave to rise again for ½ hour. Bake in a hot oven for 40 minutes to 1 hour.

Irish Soda Bread

1 lb. plain flour
¼ lb. butter
¼ lb. sugar
pinch of salt
1 teaspoon cream of tartar
½ lb. sultanas
2 oz. chopped peel
½ pint (generous) sour milk
1 teaspoon bicarbonate of soda

Sieve dry ingredients together. Rub in butter until like fine breadcrumbs. Stir in sugar and fruit. Add the milk and mix to a soft dough. Knead slightly. Place in a greased loaf tin and bake in a hot oven for one hour, turn down heat to moderate and bake for further ½ hour. Cool before cutting. Slice and butter.

Sultana and Treacle Bread

½ lb. wholemeal flour
1 oz. butter
¼ oz. sugar
2 oz. sultanas
pinch of salt
¼ oz. fresh yeast
1 tablespoon treacle
¼ pint boiling water
1 oz. candied peel

Place the water and treacle in a large bowl. Cream the yeast and sugar. Add the yeast mixture to the water and treacle. Add the dry ingredients, then the fruit. Knead well. Allow to rise for one hour. Knock down again, and leave to rise again in a greased loaf tin for ½ hour. Brush top with milk and sugar. Bake in hot oven for ½ hour.

Home Made Bread

4 lbs plain flour
pinch of salt
½ lb. potatoes
1 pint home made yeast
warm water to mix

Home made yeast can be made as follows :

1 small handful hops
1 tablespoon salt
3 tablespoons sugar
3 pints water
1 tablespoon flour
2 large potatoes

Boil hops in the water for one hour. Strain. Mix sugar, salt and flour. Pour half of the hot liquid onto the sugar mixture. Stir well. Grate potatoes, pour remaining liquid over the potatoes and stir until it becomes like the consistency of thick cream. Add the two mixtures together and keep in bottles — only half fill bottles. Cork and leave for about 3-4 days before using.

Cook potatoes and put through a sieve. Sift flour and add salt, the potatoes and enough water to make a smooth dough. Cover and leave overnight in a warm spot. Next day divide into three loaves and knead again. Place in greased loaf tins and place to rise again for ½ hour. Bake in hot oven for 1 hour. Cool on wire rack.

MANX

Fruit Bonnag

    1 lb. self-raising flour
    1 oz. butter
    handful currants, sultanas, mixed peel and raisins
    1 oz. lard
    2 oz. sugar
    milk to mix

Rub fat into flour. Mix in fruit and sugar. Add milk to make a soft dough. Cook in a flat meat tin in a moderate oven until browned and cooked.

Bunloaf

    12 oz. plain flour
    3 oz. lard
    ½ teaspoon mixed spice
    6 oz. brown sugar
    ½ teaspoon nutmeg
    2 oz. mixed peel
    8 oz. currants
    1 level teaspoon black treacle
    3 oz. butter
    pinch of salt
    4 tablespoons buttermilk
    ½ teaspoon bicarbonate of soda
    8 oz. sultanas
    2 oz. raisins
    2 eggs

Place flour and salt in a bowl. Add fats and rub in well. Stir in mixed spice, nutmeg, bicarbonate of soda, sugar and peel. Add treacle to eggs and buttermilk and beat well. Add to dry ingredients and add fruit. Place in a greased loaf tin and bake in a moderate oven for 2½ hours. Leave to cool in the tin.

Babs

    1 lb. plain flour
    2 oz. melted butter
    ½ oz. yeast
    1 egg
    1 teaspoon salt
    ½ pint warm milk
    ½ oz. sugar

Mix the yeast and sugar until liquid. Pour melted butter into yeast mixture. Add warmed milk. Make a well in the flour mixture and add the yeast mixture and the well beaten egg. Allow to prove until double in size. Cut up into small pieces and shape. Allow to prove again for about an hour. Bake in hot oven for about 15-20 minutes.

Oatcakes

    2 cups fine oatmeal
    pinch of salt
    pinch of bicarbonate of soda
    ½ oz. beef dripping
    8 oz. hot water

Mix dry ingredients together. Rub in the dripping. Mix with the water to a pastry dough consistency. Roll out on a floured board. Cut into squares and cook on a hot griddle.

Scottish Bannock

This is almost like a fruit cake and was reputed to be one of Queen Victoria's favourite tea-time treats.

    2½ lbs plain flour
    ¼ lb. melted butter
    4 oz. brown sugar
    4 oz. sultanas
    3 oz. candied peel
    pinch of salt
    1¼ pint warmed milk
    1 oz. yeast
    1 oz. sugar
    3 oz. hazelnuts/walnuts
    few almonds for decoration

Mix the yeast and sugar until a liquid. Add half the warmed milk. Add the melted butter. Sift the flour and mix in the fruit. Add the yeast mixture and the rest of the milk to the flour and fruit mixture.
Leave in a warm place to double in size. Knead well and put into a large round tin which has been well greased. Sprinkle almonds over the top of cake.
Bake in moderate oven for about 45-50 minutes.
Leave for 1 day before cutting. Slice and spread with butter.

Bara Cymraeg

2 lbs. white flour
1 lb. brown flour
1 oz. yeast
1 oz. sugar
1 oz. butter
½ oz. salt
30 oz. warm water

Mix yeast and sugar. Add the butter to the warm water. Mix flour and salt in a large bowl. Add the yeast, sugar and water to the flour. Mix to a dough. Grease the bread tins. Half fill the tins. Leave to prove in warm place. Bake in hot oven. Mark 6 Gas, 400° F. Electricity for 35-40 minutes.

Bara Brith *(made with yeast)*

1½ lb. plain flour
pinch salt
2 oz. butter
1 teaspoon mixed spice
1 egg
½ oz. yeast
4 oz. sugar
½ pint milk and water
4 oz. sultanas
4 oz. currants
4 oz. candied peel
1 oz. stoned raisins

Cream yeast and sugar. Heat the milk/water mixture to luke warm, mix in with the yeast. Mix flour, spice and salt. Make a well in the centre and pour in the yeast mixture. Stir. Cover with a cloth and leave in a warm place to prove for 30 minutes. Melt the butter. Add to the gently proving yeast mixture. Sprinkle with some extra flour. Leave for another half hour. Beat the egg and add to the dough. Knead well, stir in the fruit. Turn mixture onto floured board. Grease 2 lb. loaf tin. Place mixture in tins (makes enough for two tins). Leave to prove again for ½ hour. Bake in hot oven for 15 minutes. Turn heat down to moderate and cook for another 35 minutes. Cool on a wire tray. Leave for one day before eating. Slice and butter.

Bara Brith *(without yeast)*

2 lbs. self raising flour
2 lbs. mixed dried fruit
4 tbs. marmalade
2 eggs
12 tablespoons sugar
1 pint warm tea (strained)
2 tablespoons ground mixed spice
Honey for glazing

Mix flour and dried fruit. Add marmalade, beaten eggs, sugar and spice to the warm tea. Add the liquid to the dry mixture and mix well. Line and grease 4 loaf tins. Place mixture into the tins. Bake in a moderate oven for 1½ hours. Cool on wire racks. Store for one day before cutting.

Bara Ceirch

These are similar to the Scottish oatcakes but they are thinner.

½ lb. fine oatmeal
1 oz. lard
1 oz. butter
½ oz. sugar
¾ cup warm water
(boil the water and leave to cool for 5 minutes.)

Add the fats to the water. Mix in the salt, sugar and oatmeal. Make into a soft dough. Sprinkle oatmeal

on a board and flatten with the palm of the hands. Place onto a hot bakestone or a "llechfaen" as it is called in Cardiganshire, to harden. Bake the oatcakes for about 5-7 minutes on each side on a griddle.

These oatcakes are not the easiest to make, but well worth mastering. Keep in an airtight tin.

Crempog

4 oz. self raising flour
2 oz. sugar
4 tablespoons buttermilk
1 teaspoon bicarbonate soda
2 teaspoons cream of tartar
7 oz. milk
4 eggs
butter for frying
pinch of salt

Add the bicarbonate of soda, salt and cream of tartar to the flour. Beat eggs. Add the eggs to the milk. Make a well in the flour. Mix the flour and liquid together. Heat butter in a cast iron fry pan. Spoon mixture into pan and cook till golden on both sides. Serve warm, buttered and sprinkled with sugar. Honey is also good on Crempog

---

Fish

Sole Bonne Femme

2 lbs. sole fillets
½ cup mushrooms
½ cup shallots
1 cup dry white wine
pinch chopped parsley
4 medium tomatoes
salt and pepper
1 cup cream

Use a wide bottomed pan for this dish as it will then be easier to cook the fish without breaking the fillets.

Place the shallots, mushrooms, a sprinkle of the parsley and seasonings on the bottom of the pan. Put the fish on top and pour the wine over. Cover and simmer very gently for 5 minutes or until the fish flakes easily when prodded with a fork. Take out the fish when cooked and place on a platter and keep hot. Add the cream to the pan and boil until reduced by about a quarter. Be very careful not to cook too long, as sauce will burn easily. Pour over the fish and serve with more parsley and tomato slices.

Serve with new boiled potatoes and a green salad.

Fish Terrine

½ lb. shrimps or prawns
½ lb. halibut
½ teaspoon salt
2 teaspoons lemon juice
2 teaspoons white dry wine
¼ teaspoon fresh black pepper
¼ teaspoon tarragon
¼ teaspoon fresh chopped parsley
¼ cup chopped green shallots
¼ cup butter
¼ cup plain flour
1¼ cups cream (top of milk will do)
2 well beaten eggs

Blend the cooked fish in an electric blender until quite smooth. Keep the white and pink fish separate. Melt the butter and fry the shallots until soft. Add the seasonings. Blend the flour with the wine and lemon juice into a smooth paste. Add to shallots, take from heat and add the cream. Add the beaten eggs and stir well. Mix enough of the sauce with the fish (still separate) to make into a runny mixture. Pour half the white fish mixture into a greased terrine (6-8 cup size) then add the pink fish, then the white. Chop up finely some pink salmon and place on top. This will sink into the sauce mixture a little and add colour to the terrine. Cover the dish and stand in a large container of boiling water and bake for 30-40 minutes in a moderate oven. Remove and chill.

Serve with thin brown bread slices.

Creamed Halibut and Sorrell

1 lb. halibut fillets
2 oz. butter
½ cup green shallots (chopped)
4 tablespoons dry white wine
1½ - 1¾ cup chopped sorrell
1 oz. butter
1 oz. plain flour
½ cup cream
seasonings
pinch cinnamon, nutmeg and some chopped parsley
½ pint good fish stock

Arrange fish fillets in a pie dish on top of the melted 2 oz. butter. Sprinkle with shallots and the white wine. Cover and cook until the fish flakes. Melt the 1 oz. butter in a pan and add flour. Blend with the seasonings until smooth. Add fish stock and cook. Add the chopped sorrell and cream and warm without boiling. Pour over the fish cutlets and serve at once.

Fish Gazy Pie

8 herrings or mackerel
2 oz. breadcrumbs
4 oz. cream
parsley
few drops vinegar
4 eggs
salt and pepper
3 uncooked potatoes
sufficient pastry to cover the top of a piedish

Clean and bone the fish : leave the heads on. Grease a pie dish. Grate the potatoes and arrange to form a base. Place the fish on top with their heads towards the centre. Season with the salt, pepper and vinegar. Beat the eggs and cream and pour over the fish. Lay the pastry on top and leave a hole in the centre to allow the heads of the fish to poke out. Bake for 1 hour in moderate oven. Place a sprig of parsley on each fish head.

Singing Snails

12 snails
some garlic
salt and pepper
1 oz. butter

Drop snails into boiling water and boil for ½ hr. Take off shells and cut away the hard meats. Put meat into a greased pie dish : cover with the butter pats and season. Cook for 10 mins in hot oven. Serve with thin brown bread.

Potted Shrimps

1 pint shrimps
pinch nutmeg
salt and pepper
4 oz. butter
pinch garlic powder
1 oz. white wine or sweet cider

Heat butter and add the prepared shrimps. Add wine and other ingredients. Heat gently but do not boil. Pot and eat cold with green salad.

Lampreys

These are rather similar to eels and according to some of the early monarchs of England were considered a great delicacy. The end product certainly tastes very much better than the raw product looks.

Lampreys

> approx 2 lbs of lampreys
> salt and pepper
> juice of 1 lemon
> small chopped onion
> ½ pint dry white wine
> pinch nutmeg

Clean and gut the fish. Place in a piedish. Season well and pour over the wine. Cook with the lid on for about 2 hrs. or until tender, in a slow oven.

MANX

Manx Kippers

> 2 kippers
> 1 oz. butter

Place the kippers on a shallow dish. Dot with butter and grill for about 3-4 minutes. Serve hot with thin brown bread.

Queenies with a Cheese and Onion Sauce

    10 queenies
    2 small onions
    ½ pint fish stock
    seasonings
    Sauce :
    ½ oz. butter
    ½ pint milk
    ½ oz. flour
    4 oz. Cheddar cheese
    1 diced cooked onion

Place the shelled Queenies in an ovenproof dish. Add stock and onion. Season and bake in moderate oven for about ¼ hour. Lift the scallops out of the dish and replace in their shells. Make the sauce and serve by pouring a little over each shell. Brown under grill.

Manx Herrings and Priddhas

    Allow two herrings per person
    Allow two medium potatoes per person
    1 raw onion (sliced)

Scrub the potatoes and place in water to par boil. Lay the fish on top of the potatoes and cook fish. Drain potatoes and lift out fish carefully. Serve with raw onion rings and plenty of buttermilk to drink.

This is an old traditional Manx rhyme about this famous recipe :

I'm a native of Peel
And I think for a meal,
That there's nothin' like priddhas and herrin'
I was reared on the quay
An' I followed the say,
An' its 'mighty good fishin' I'm gettin'.

The Tanrogans are the large scallops caught around the Island. The smaller ones are called Queenies. It is now much easier to purchase the Queenies from the local fishmongers.

Grilled Sole

    1 fillet of sole
    seasonings
    1 beaten egg
    4 oz. small mushrooms (sliced)
    2 oz. butter
    brown breadcrumbs

Melt butter in a flat frypan. Cup up sole fillet into fingers. Dip in butter, egg and breadcrumbs and cook in the butter till golden brown. Cook the sliced mushrooms in and around the sole fingers. Serve with a green salad.

Irish Crab

    2 crabs (cooked)
    ½ cup fresh cream
    salt and pepper
    1 cup mayonnaise
    chopped parsley
    lemon juice

Arrange the lettuce in a salad bowl to form a base for the crab. Take out all the meat from the shells. Mix the cream and mayonnaise together. Add the parsley and season. Pile the crab meat onto the lettuce leaves.

Shellfish is readily available in most parts of Ireland, but around the Dublin area shell fish is really not considered a delicacy, but simply one of the foods that the Emerald Isle provides for its people to eat and enjoy.

Scallops in a Cheese and Mushroom Sauce

    8 – 10 medium sized scallops
    2 tbs. breadcrumbs
    ½ lb. button mushrooms
    1 oz. flour
    ½ cup cream
    ¼ lb. sharp cheese
    salt and pepper
    2 small onions
    2 oz. butter
    ½ pint milk
    4 dessertspoons sherry

Simmer the scallops in the milk until cooked. Keep the milk. Remove from the shells and cut into thick slices. Melt the butter and add the chopped onion. Add flour and stir to ensure there are no lumps. Add the heated milk, cream and sherry. Season. Add the cooked chopped mushrooms. Pile into scallop shells and cut a slice of butter to top each of the shells. Grill until the cheese browns.

Creamed Haddie

1 lb. Haddock fillets
¾ pint white sauce
½ lb. fresh mushrooms
2 oz. grated cheese
salt and pepper
3 skinned tomatoes

Grease a pie dish. Cover the base with the fish fillets. Slice the mushrooms and sprinkle over the fish. Put the tomatoes on top of the mushrooms. Pour over the white sauce and sprinkle the cheese over the top. Bake in a moderate oven for about ½ hour or until the fillets are tender and the top brown.

Lobster in Shells

1 lobster
¼ lb. grated cheese
½ pint white sauce
¼ pint single cream
butter
salt and pepper

Remove all meat from the lobster. Make sure the shell is intact as the fish is served in the half shells.

Add the lobster meat to the sauce and half the cheese. Season. Place the mixture back into the cleaned shells. Pour the cream over the fish and sprinkle with the remaining cheese. Bake in hot oven until hot enough and cheese is bubbly on top. Serve with fresh crusty bread.

Tweed Salmon

About 2 lbs salmon
sweet white wine
2 oz. chopped shallots or chives
pt. water or fish stock (if not enought liquid from wine)
salt and pepper
parsley

Place salmon in enough water to cover. Poach gently for about 5-10 minutes. Cool. Flake the meat off the bones. Place in an ovenproof serving dish. Sprinkle shallots over and cover with the wine. Season. Bake for about ½ hour in a moderate oven. Serve hot or cold. If serving cold, serve with a cucumber sauce.

Eog wedi ei Bobi *(Baked Salmon)*

4 lb. Salmon
4 oz. butter
pinch of rosemary
nutmeg,
salt and pepper
a few cloves
1 teaspoon vinegar
1 teaspoon lemon juice

Clean the fish. Rub inside and out with the mixed seasonings. Grease a large oven proofed dish and place the fish in it. Cover with dots of butter and roast in a moderate oven for 20 minutes to the pound. Baste frequently.

Serve on a warmed dish with wedges of lemon.

Mussel Stew

Approx. 2 quarts mussels
1 oz. butter
1 cup water
Clove of garlic (wild garlic grown in abundance in Wales)
2 small finely grated onions
4 oz. white breadcrumbs
teaspoon lemon juice
teaspoon chopped fresh parsley
salt and pepper
½ glass sweet madeira wine
egg yolk
½ cup small button mushrooms
¼ cup fresh cream

Wash and clean the mussels. Place in a saucepan and cook for 5 minutes or till the shells are open. Strain the liquid and keep. Break up the mussel shells and remove the beards. Fry the onion in the butter and mushrooms if using. Add the breadcrumbs, seasonings, juices and the other ingredients. Simmer for about 3-4 minutes but do not boil. Now add the egg yolk and cream (mixed together) stir in the mussels. Heat but do not boil as egg will curdle

Mussels are a firm favourite in the Swansea area and the market there is famous for its fresh fish supplies.

Pastai Gocos *(Cockle Pie)*

The Gower area is the home of the shell fish of Wales.
This is only one of the hundreds of recipes from that
area.

Clean the cockles. Place in large pan and cover with
water. Boil till the shells open. Remove the cockles
from the shells. Keep some of the cockle stock.

    Pastry :
    12 oz. short crust pastry
    Pie filling :
    5 cups cockles
    ¾ lb. streaky bacon
    ½ pint cockle stock
    2 small white onions
    2 shallots, cut up
    seasoning
    just enough milk to glaze

Line pie dish with pastry. Fill with mixture and seal
top. Glaze with milk. Bake in moderate to hot oven
for ½ — ¾ hour.
    Serve hot or cold.

Cig Moch a Brithyll *(Bacon & Trout)*

    8 medium sized trout
    16 rashers streaky bacon
    salt and pepper
    ½ oz. butter

Clean the fish and remove the bones. Grease an oven
proofed dish. Line the base with half the bacon
rashers. Place trout on top and cover with the
remaining bacon. Season. Dot with butter. Bake in
a hot oven for 20 minutes.
    Serves 8.

main COURSES

Veal Rolls

 2 lbs. veal (pound very thin)
 1 lb. chopped lean bacon
 1 cup white wine
 1 oz. butter
 1 oz. flour
 2 cloves crushed garlic
 1 oz. chopped fresh parsley
 1 cup chicken broth
 salt and black pepper
 pinch thyme
 1 cup chopped onion
 1 bay leaf

Cut meat into eight square pieces and pound to about 1/16th inch. Mix bacon, onions and seasonings together and place a small amount of the mixture on the veal squares. Roll and tie with string. Melt butter in a pan and brown the rolls. Place onto the bottom of an oven dish. Pour a little of the wine over rolls and cook in a moderate to hot oven for about ¾ hour or until meat is tender. Make a gravy with the remainder of the ingredients. Season and serve poured over the rolls.

These rolls are delicious if served with red cabbage and soured cream.

Normandy Beef

 3 lb. piece of beef fillet
 1½ lb. rich short pastry
 1 beaten egg
 1½ lb. mushrooms
 4 oz. butter
 seasonings
 2 small onions

Trim all fat from meat. Place in a roasting dish and "undercook". Take out and chill — preferably overnight. Make pastry as follows :

 1 lb. butter
 6 cups plain flour
 good pinch of salt
 4 tablespoons of water
 4 tablespoons of lemon juice

Rub butter and flour until like fine breadcrumbs. Mix with water and lemon juice to a dough. Chill for 1 hour. Roll out pastry long and wide enough to cover the piece of meat. Chop onions and mushrooms and cook in the butter until the onions are transparent and the mushrooms soft. Make a pocket slit in the middle of the piece of beef and fill with half the mushrooms. Place meat on rolled out pastry and surround with the remaining mushrooms and onions. Season well and close the pastry case. Glaze with the

beaten egg. Cook in hot oven for about ¾ hour to
1 hour or until the pastry is a golden brown in colour.

Serve hot with a good sauce, e.g. mushroom or
horseradish sauce.

CORNISH

Devon Pork and Cider

1 lb. pork fillet
2 oz. flour
seasonings
pinch cinnamon
4 small cooking apples
2 oz. butter
2 - 3 oz. cream
1 pint sweet cider
1 stick celery
½ lb. onions
parsley

Cut the meat into cubes, and toss in the flour. Heat
the butter in a large pan, and add the meat : gently
brown. Add all the chopped vegetables and other
ingredients. Transfer to an ovenproof dish. Cook in
moderate oven for about one hour. Just before
serving stir in the cream. Sprinkle with chopped
parsley.

Cornish Pasty

1 lb. lean trimmed mutton
3 good sized potatoes (chopped)
2 medium chopped onions
2 medium chopped carrots
pinch chopped parsley
pinch chopped fresh herbs
salt and pepper
1 lb. shortcrust pastry

Make the pastry and chill for about an hour before
using. Chop up the meat finely, mix in the chopped
vegetables with the meat, herbs and season well.
Roll out pastry to a large round. Place meat and
vegetable mixture in the centre. Bring over one side
of the pastry to form a half round. Crimp edges and
glaze with milk. Bake in a moderately hot oven for
1 hour. Filling for a Cornish pasty should always be
raw.

This cornish pasty can be made as one large one or
several small ones. In Cornwall they were eaten by
the Tin and Copper miners at "Crib" time.

Colcannon

This is one of the traditional Irish dishes using the much favoured potato. It was often served on Halloween and also as a supper dish of "First Kettling Night" — the first day that friends visited the home of a newly married couple.

    1 lb. cooked mashed potatoes
    ½ lb. bacon (cut into small cubes)
    ½ lb. shredded cabbage
    ½ lb. onions (chopped)
    salt and pepper
    pinch of parsley
    2 oz. dripping

Melt the dripping and add the vegetables. Cook until browned. Add the bacon and cook. Season. Serve on a large platter with parsley sprinkled over the top.

Irish Stew

    2 lb. neck of mutton
    3 lb. potatoes
    1 lb. onions
    ½ pint water
    salt and pepper

Cube the meat and cup up the vegetables into small pieces. Place in a large saucepan and add the stock. Season. Simmer for 3 hours.

   The meat used in the original Irish Stew was, I gather, that of a goat or kid, but now it seems to be mutton that is used for this very old Irish dish.

Isle of Man Hot Pot

    Large neck of mutton
    1 lb. onions
    2 lbs. potatoes
    water to cover
    ½ lb. leeks
    ½ lb. carrots
    seasonings

Place meat on base of large pot. Cover over and around with the vegetables. Season and cover with water. Simmer gently for 3 - 3½ hours.

The Tinkers Dinner

How this recipe came by its odd name I do not know.
Maybe it was because the Irish tinkers are supposed
to be very light fingered! This dish is now served at
festivals, like Harvest time and of course Christmas
time.

    1 turkey
    Stuffing :
    1 lb. dry breadcrumbs
    1 lb. diced onions
    4 tablespoons mashed potatoes
    pinch of sage
    ½ teaspoon salt
    ½ teaspoon black pepper
    1 beaten egg
    water to mix

Mix all the stuffing and put into the turkey. Secure
the back and tail so that the stuffing does not ooze
out. Place the turkey in a roasting dish and brush
with melted butter. Cook for 15 — 20 minutes to
the lb. in a moderate oven. This dish can be served
with potato pancakes :

    1 lb. grated raw potatoes
    salt and pepper
    2 oz. flour
    2 beaten eggs
    2 small chopped onions

Mix the potato, onion, egg and flour together.
Season. Shape into fritters. Fry until cooked a
golden brown.

Sollaghan

Take a basinful of oatmeal. Put meal into oven or in
pan on fire and keep turning meal until it is crisped
to a reddish colour. Put meal into a dish : add salt
and pepper and a lump of butter to flavour. Then
put 2 - 3 basinfuls of stock or broth upon the meal
and mix until it sticks together in lumps. Fill up
dish with broth until enough to serve into plates
upon the table to eat. This makes a very wholesome
meal for men. Sollaghan was traditionally served on
the Island on Christmas morning.

Aberdeen Sausage

    1 lb. stewing steak (minced)
    ½ lb. minced streaky bacon
    ¼ lb. rolled oats
    1 beaten egg
    1 tablespoon Worcestershire sauce
    ¼ lb. breadcrumbs
    . seasonings

Mix the meats, breadcrumbs and seasonings together.
Bind with the egg. Make into a roll. Bake in a
moderate oven for about 1½ - 2 hours or until meat
is cooked through. Leave to cool. Use next day,
sliced with a salad.

Scotch Eggs

    6 hard boiled eggs (shelled)
    1 lb. sausagemeat
    seasonings
    breadcrumbs

Cover the eggs with the breadcrumbs. Cut up the
seasoned sausage meat into 6 sections. Cover each
egg with enough of the meat. Fry in deep fat.
Serve hot or cold.

Haggis

    the liver, heart and lights of one sheep
    ½ lb. suet
    large cup of fine oatmeal
    2 large onions
    salt and pepper
    few drops of milk

Put the liver etc., in a large pan and cover with water.
Simmer for 1½ hours. Toast the oatmeal. Cool the
meats. When cold mince roughly. Chop onions and
mix in the oatmeal. Season. Add a little milk if too
dry. Place in a large basin. Cover with foil and steam
for about 3 - 4 hours. Serve hot.

Potes Mis Medi *(Harvest Hot Pot)*

½ lb. bacon pieces
½ lb. cubed lamb (uncooked)
1 lb. potatoes
1 lb. carrots
1 lb. onions
4 leeks
2 pints water
½ lb. swedes or turnips
1 oz. butter
1 oz. wheaten flour
seasonings

In a large pot, melt the butter, fry and brown meats. Peel and cube all the vegetables. Add the vegetables, seasoning and water. Simmer gently for two hours. Serve with fresh brown bread.

This is a complete meal in one pot.

This dish was often used during the potato picking season in Wales as it was easily made and left on the hook over the open fire to keep hot. The pickers were often late in to their dinners — often from chatting — not from picking the potatoes.

There used to be a school holiday in Wales called Wythnos Hela Tatws (Potato Picking Week).

Ham in Cider

The ham should be soaked overnight in cold water.

5 - 6 lb. piece of ham
1¼ pint cider and water (½ quantities of each)
juice of 1 lemon
1 large onion
8 cloves
pinch of brown sugar

Place the ham into a large stewpan. Prick the onion with the cloves : add all other ingredients. Bring to the boil and simmer slowly for 25 — 30 minutes, to each pound. Cool, then peel off the skin.

Mix together :
3 tablespoons brown sugar
3 tablespoons breadcrumbs
1 teaspoon made mustard
¼ teaspoon mace
¼ teaspoon nutmeg

Press the mixture into the ham and place into a greased pie dish. Bake for 40 — 50 minutes in moderate oven. Serve with vegetables or salad.
Can also be served with the traditional parsley sauce.

Ffagots

2 lbs. of either calves, pigs or lambs liver
5 oz. finely chopped suet
5 oz. oatmeal or breadcrumbs
3 large onions (minced)
2 teaspoons salt
¼ teaspoon black pepper
pinch each of nutmeg, sage, thyme, mace.

Place all the ingredients into a large bowl and mix very thoroughly. Grease a large meat tin and place mixture into this. Cover the top with pork flat pieces.

Cook in a slow oven for about an hour. After ½ hour mark top of meat into squares. Leave to get cold in the tin. Can be eaten cold or hot.

This recipe was much used by the families of miners, as the fagots were so easily transportable in their miners "tocyn" (lunch). They also provided vital nourishment for the strenuous work of mining.

Ffest y Cybydd

1 lb. streaky bacon
1 lb. potatoes
1 large swede
1 leek
4 onions
½ lb. carrots
salt and pepper
½ pint stock

Cut up the vegetables into slices. Dice the leek and bacon. Place alternative layers of bacon and the vegetables. Season to taste. Pour stock over. Bake in a moderate oven for 1 hour.

This dish, with fresh bread, was often served at my home.

game

Brittany Chicken

    1 large roasting chicken (5 lbs.)
    seasonings
    1 oz. butter
    1 oz. plain flour
    2 lbs. small onions
    2 cups water/white win

Melt the butter and peel onions. Fry in the butter until golden. Clean the fat off the chicken and season outside. Stuff the inside with the onions. Secure the skin with a thread. Place in a roasting dish and cook for about 1½-2 hours, with the wine/water poured around it. Thicken the liquid with some flour and season.

    Serve with new potatoes, carrots and green salad.

Rabbit with Mushrooms

    1 medium sized fresh rabbit
    1 lb. mushrooms (cleaned and sliced)
    2 cups white wine
    2 oz. butter
    chopped parsley
    1 clove garlic (crushed or chopped)
    1 lb. small white onions
    seasonings
    2 oz. plain flour

Cut up rabbit into about six pieces. Melt the butter and brown the rabbit pieces. Thicken the fat with the flour when meat is browned. Add mushrooms, onions, white wine and seasonings, and cook until rabbit meat is tender in a slow oven.

    Serve sprinkled with chopped parsley.

Quail in Red Wine

    8 quailes
    2 oz. butter
    2 oz. plain flour
    1 cup beef stock
    ½ cup sherry
    black pepper
    ½ pint red wine
    salt
    a few grapes to decorate

Clean the birds. Tie the birds across their breasts with a piece of white string — this keeps them in shape

whilst cooking. Melt the butter and brown the quails.
Transfer to a large casserole and add the sherry, wine
and seasonings. Cook until tender in a moderate oven
with the lid on for all but the last half hour or so.
Thicken the gravy juices with the flour and serve hot.
At least two quails per person is needed as they are
very tiny birds.

CORNISH

Rabbit Hoggan

Pastry :
1 lb. plain flour
6 oz. lard
salt
drop of lemon juice
enough water to mix
For the filling :
1 lb rabbit meat (chopped into small pieces)
The rabbit must be young and fresh,
6 potatoes (small)
2 carrots
seasonings

2 onions
2 small turnips
little amount of stock

Make the pastry and roll out to a round. Cut up the
meat and vegetables into small cubes. Place the
vegetables and meat in the middle of the pastry round.
Season and just put a little stock over. Seal the pastry
and stand it on its base on a baking tray. Crimp the
edges and brush with milk. Bake for about 1-1½
hours in a moderate oven, or as the contents are
uncooked maybe a little longer. This amount makes
one huge hoggan or 6 smaller ones.

Jugged Hare

Jugged Hare was often served in the West Country on Boxing Day.

Hang the hare for 3-4 days – Joint. Place in the following marinade the day before it is to be cooked :

1 large glass sweet cider
1 large glass white vinegar
1 sliced onion
salt and pepper

¼ lb. streaky bacon
4 carrots
3 small onions
bayleaf
2 small glasses of red wine
little drop of port
seasonings
2 oz. butter
2 oz. arrowroot
approx. 1 pint good brown stock or use the marinade

Peel and chop the vegetables. Melt butter and brown vegetables. Coat hare in flour, add to the pan. Cook until slightly browned. Transfer vegetables to a large pie dish. Place hare pieces on top. Pour wines and stock over and cook with the lid on for about 3 hours in a moderate oven. Thicken with the arrowroot if the sauce is too thin. Just before serving add about 2 tablespoons of redcurrant jelly.

Roast Grouse

2 young grouse
½ lb. stewing meat (beef preferably)
½ lb. streaky bacon
2 oz. butter
seasonings

Cut the steak into four equal pieces. Wash and dry the grouse and put the steak inside the birds (2 pieces in each bird). Place the grouse in a buttered dish to roast and put the bacon strips over them. Roast in a medium oven for about an hour. Serve the steak together with the birds. Sufficient for 4 people.

Stewed Rabbit

1 rabbit
½ lb. streaky bacon
½ lb. potatoes
½ lb. onions
½ lb. leeks
seasonings
2 oz. flour
2 oz. butter
½ lb. carrots
½ lb. turnips
1 pint stock
chopped parsley

Cut the rabbit into 6 portions. Melt the butter. Coat the rabbit pieces in flour. Fry until browned. Cut up the vegetables and place over the meat in a large stewpot. Add stock and season. Cook slowly for about 2 hours.

Serve this stew with some dumplings and it is a complete meal in one pot.

2 oz. flour
2 eggs
2 oz. butter
½ pint boiling water
(if not boiling in the stew)

Melt the butter. Add to the flour and salt. Beat the eggs and add to the dry mixture. Roll into small balls. Cook in the boiling water or add to the stew about 10 minutes before serving. These are better tasting if cooked in the stewpot.

Roasted Hare

The times for roasting a young hare is about 20 minutes to the pound.

Prepare the hare and remove its head. Leave a longish piece of neck skin for trussing and to keep the stuffing in. Stuff the hare with the following :

4 oz. white breadcrumbs
2 oz. butter
seasonings

1 beaten egg
2 chopped medium onions
pinch of sage and thyme

Add these together and use for the stuffing. Sew the hare with a thick cotton which can be easily removed before serving. Place hare in a roasting dish; cover with strips of bacon. Cook in a moderate oven. Serve with roast carrots and potatoes and a gravy made from the roasted hare juices.

MANX

Roast Chicken with Sage and Onion Stuffing

1 roasting fowl
3 potatoes
3 carrots
3 medium onions
Bacon fat (strips)
Stuffing :
¼ lb. stale bread (crumbled)
2 large chopped onions
pinch sage
2 oz. butter
salt and pepper
little water

Clean the chicken and remove the inards. Pour some water over the bread to soak. Chop onion. Mix in the sage and season. Peel and chop up the other vegetables and cook meat. Mash all together with some butter. Add to stuffing mixture and stuff the fowl. Cook in a large roasting pan in moderate oven for 15 minutes to the pound and fifteen minutes over. Serve with roast carrots, potatoes and a green vegetable. Make gravy with the fowl juices from the roasting pan.

Scotsman Casserole

brace of grouse
2 oz. butter
2 small onions (chopped)
4 rashers streaky bacon
½ lb. fried mushrooms (sliced)
¼ pint red wine
¼ pint water
2 small carrots (diced)
salt and pepper

Prepare the grouse and cut in half. Heat butter in a large pan and brown birds well. Place in an ovenproof casserole and add carrots, onions, mushrooms and bacon (chopped). Season. Add the wine and water. Cook in moderate oven for 2 - 2½ hours or until tender. Thicken the gravy before serving with flour, if needed.

The Huntsmans Dinner

1 boiling chicken
1 lb. streaky bacon
½ lb. carrots
2 pints of stock
Seasonings
1 Rabbit
1 lb. potatoes
½ lb. onions
parsley

Cut up the chicken and rabbit into small portions. Melt butter in a large cook pot. Coat meats with flour and fry until brown. Cut up vegetables and add to the meat. Add stock. Cook for about two hours on a simmering heat. Serve with a green vegetable.

Montgomeryshire Pheasant

1 pheasant
1 oz. butter
1 large onion
1 large carrot
1 large leek
1 turnip
pinch of parsley, thyme, salt and pepper
water
¼ bottle of red wine
1 oz. flour

Prepare the pheasant. Heat the butter in a heavy pan. Lightly fry the bird till browned. Take out and put to one side. Peel and cut up vegetables into small cubes or slices. Place in bottom of pan and add seasonings. Place the pheasant onto the vegetables and cover with wine and water. Place a lid on the pot and simmer slowly for two hours. Thicken with the flour just before serving.
  Serves 4.

Pastai Cwningen

1 jointed and cooked rabbit
8 slices streaky bacon
1 onion
1 large leek
1 pint of good stock
salt and pepper to taste
butter for browning the meat
Make up short crust pastry using :
8 oz. flour
4 oz. butter
1 egg
2 tablespoons water
pinch of salt

Line a fairly large deep pie dish with the pastry. Heat butter and fry the rabbit till browned all over. Add the bacon, onion and leek, also seasoning. Let this cook and when cold, place into pastry case. Add stock and place the crust over the top. Seal and brush with egg or milk. Bake in a moderate oven for 30 minutes till pastry is browned.
  Serves 4 - 6.

Twrci Mewn Blanced

    1 lb. cold turkey — cut up in small cubes
    4 small onions
    1 leek
    1 carrot
    1 swede or turnip
    4 potatoes
    salt and pepper to taste
    ½ pint good giblet stock
    Make a quantity of hot water pastry as follows:
    ½ lb. flour
    1 gill milk
    pinch of salt
    2 oz. lard
    1 gill water

Line a dish with the warm pastry. Place into the shell the diced turkey meat, onion and the other vegetables cut up small, add seasoning and stock. Seal the case and bake in moderate oven till browned and vegetables cooked. About 1 hour.

Serves 4.

This is a favourite dish in Cardiganshire to use up the Christmas turkey.

Salted Duck

The duck must be salted one day before being cooked.

    1 large duck
    1 lb. small onions
    1 oz. flour
    1 oz. butter
    ¾ pint milk
    salt and pepper

Place the duck in a pot and cover with water. Simmer slowly for 1½ - 2 hours, depending on size. Boil the onion in the milk till tender. Make a roux sauce by melting butter, stir in flour and seasoning and add to milk and onions. Drain the duck and place on a large platter. Pour over sauce.

Serve with new Pembrokeshire boiled potatoes, carrots and a green vegetable.

Serves 6.

This is a very old and a traditional Welsh recipe.

Gwydd y Dolig

12-14 lb. goose
6 tablespoons lard
4 tablespoons red wine, maderia or port
8 strips streaky bacon
The stuffing :
6 oz. white breadcrumbs
2 peeled and chopped apples
2 small peeled and chopped onions
1 egg
salt and pepper
pinch sage and nutmeg

Make the stuffing. Stuff the goose and secure with a steel skewer or sew with tacking thread. Place the bird in a large baking tin. Pour over wine or port and roast in a moderate oven for 20-25 minutes to the pound. Baste often to keep moist. About ½ hour before cooking is complete place strips of bacon across the bird and leave till being served. Make in a criss-cross pattern.

This recipe is usually served with an apple sauce (as goose is a fairly fatty meat).

Sauce :
¾ lb. sharp cooking apples
3 tablespoons sugar
3 tablespoons breadcrumbs
2 small chopped onions
¾ cup cider
pinch mustard, salt and pepper
small pinch nutmeg and cinnamon

Cook the apples and onions and seasoning in the cider. When vegetables ar soft add breadcrumbs. Simmer gently for a few seconds. Serve in a gravy boat alongside the goose gravy.

This dish is served at Christmas time but occasionally at such events as christenings and weddings too.

The goose is a popular bird to keep on the small holdings in Wales, as apart from the meat the bird provides, the feathers are used for the down quilts and in years gone by the filling of the feather beds.

The long wing pinion was used for sweeping the hearth and I can recall my grandmother using one in her farm when I was young.

sweets

French Apple Tart

Short Pastry
2 cups plain flour
2 egg yolks
¾ cup butter
pinch salt

Rub butter and flour together. Add salt and egg yolks. Mix to a dough and knead for about 5 minutes.

Peel and core 1 lb. apples and slice thinly. Line a dish with half the pastry (½ lb. approximately). Layer the apple slices on top of the pastry and arrange to overlap. Sprinkle with sugar and place a few raspberries or some rasepberry jam in the centre of the tart. Cook for about ½ — ¾ hour in hot oven. When cooked glaze with whatever fruit syrup was used in the centre of the tart.

Serve hot with cream.

Chocolate Mousse

1 lb. dark chocolate
8 eggs
3 tablespoons brandy

Melt the chocolate over hot water. Add a drop of water if too thick. Stir to keep smooth. Separate egg yolks and put to one side. Stir yolks into chocolate mixture. Beat whites of eggs until very stiff. Fold the brandy into the chocolate and egg mixture and then the whites of the eggs. Leave to set in a cool place.

Pears in Red Wine

Approx. 6 medium pears
½ pint red wine
¼ cup sugar
pinch of cinnamon
1 teaspoon of Tia Maria

Peel and core the fruit. Gently pour in the wine and sugar mixture. Add the cinnamon and liqueur and heat gently. Serve hot.

Cornish Splits

    1 lb. plain flour
    ¼ pint milk
    1 oz. lard
    ½ oz. yeast
    ¼ pint water
    1 oz. butter
    1 oz. sugar
    pinch salt

Cream the sugar and yeast. Add the butter and lard to the warmed milk and water. Then add to the dry ingredients. Make into a dough. Leave to rise in warm place until well risen. Knead and shape into balls. Bake for 20 minutes in hot oven. Serve cold and split in half and fill with cream.

Golden Apples

    Approximately 1 lb. short crust pastry
    1 lb. apples
    pinch nutmeg

Roll and cut pastry into small squares. Peel and core apples. Place a quarter of the apples into a small square of pastry. Fold over into a triangle and place in a pie dish. Pour the following mixture over the pastry squares :

    1¼ boiling water
    2 oz. golden syrup
    ½ cup brown sugar

Mix well : bake in a moderate to hot oven for 40 minutes. Serve with clotted cream.

Syllabub

    4 oz. castor sugar
    juice of 2 oranges
    1 pint cream
    4 tablespoons cider
    juice of 2 lemons
    pinch of cinnamon
    4 tablespoons brandy

Grate the peel of the fruits and squeeze the juice. Mix with the cider and brandy, sugar and cinnamon and leave overnight. Next day mix in the cream and chill. Serve with fresh fruit in small glasses.

Poverty Pudding

½ cup sugar
2 cups plain flour
½ cup raisins
1 oz. peel
½ cup milk
⅓ cup boiling water
2 tablespoons treacle
2 tablespoons dripping
½ cup sultanas
1 teaspoon bicarbonate of soda
1 teaspoon mixed spice

Sift the flour, add fruit, spice and sugar. Dissolve the bicarbonate of soda in the milk. Dissolve the dripping in the boiling water. Stir into dry mixture together with the treacle. Boil in a cloth for about 2½ hours.

Baked Trifle

6 slices of stale plain cake spread with raspberry jam
1 dessertspoon sugar
2 egg yolks
2 egg whites
2 cups milk
2 drops vanilla essence
1 oz. sugar

Arrange the cake on the bottom of an ovenproof dish. Pour the milk, vanilla and beaten egg yolks over the cake. Sprinkle the sugar over the top. Bake in a moderate oven for about 1 hour, or until set. Allow to cool. Beat the egg whites until stiff. Mix in sugar and pile on top of the baked pudding. Brown in the oven for a few seconds.. Serve with cream and fresh fruit.

Moonshiners Pudding

3 tbs. cornflour
2 cups boiling water
¾ cup sugar
2 egg whites
juice of 2 lemons

Mix cornflour to a smooth paste with the lemon juice. Add sugar. Slowly pour on the boiling water. Stir well. Boil for 3 – 4 minutes. Cool, then fold in the stiffly beaten egg whites. Whisk thoroughly. Pour into a wetted mould. Chill and when set turn out onto a dish. Make a custard with the following :

2 egg yolks
1 dessertspoon sugar
vanilla essence
½ pint milk
1 teaspoon cornflour

Pour the cooled custard around the pudding.

Conemarra Tart

1 cup self-raising flour
¼ cup sugar
2 large apples
1 beaten egg
2 oz. butter
¼ cup milk
pinch of salt
½ teaspoon ground ginger
For the top :
¼ teaspoon cinnamon
¼ teaspoon nutmeg

Sift flour, ginger, salt and sugar. Rub in the fat. Add milk and eggs to make a soft dough. Roll out on a floured board. Cover the base of a greased pie dish with the pastry. Grate the apples onto the pastry. Dot with butter. Sprinkle cinnamon and nutmeg over top. Bake in a moderate oven for ½ hour. Serve hot with custard.

Irish Currant Tart

1 lb. currants
½ cup raspberry cordial
3 tablespoons gelatine
½ cup sugar
1 cooked shortcrust pastry case

Soak the currants in sufficient water to cover them overnight. Add ½ cup sugar and bring to the boil. Add the cordial and thicken with the gelatine. Leave for at least 3 hours. Fill pastry case with the mixture and serve with cream.

Manx Pudding

½ lb. plain flour
2 eggs
pinch of salt
½ pint of milk
1 oz. currants

Mix salt and flour. Make a well in the centre and add the eggs and milk. Add currants and place in a basin to steam for about 2 hours.

Binjean

1 pint fresh milk
1 teaspoon "steep" – essence of rennet

Heat milk slightly : stir in steep thoroughly and place in a dish. When cold serve with sugar and cream. A little nutmeg grated on the binjean when cold is also considered to be an improvement!

SCOTLAND

Scots Black Bun

Fruit Mixture :
1 cup plain flour
¼ lb. butter
3 eggs
1 lb. raisins
2 oz. ground almonds
1 teaspoon cream of tartar
2 oz. brown sugar
1 lb. currants
1 lb. sultanas
pinch each of baking powder, mixed spice, cinnamon, nutmeg, pepper and salt.
enough milk to mix

Mix all the dry ingredients together. Add the beaten eggs and milk to form a dough.

Pastry case :
2 cups plain flour
6 oz. butter
1 teaspoon lemon juice
water to mix

Rub the butter into the flour. Add the juice and water to form a stiff dough. Roll out thinly on a floured board and line a greased 9-10inch square tin with the pastry. Leave sufficient to cover the top. Place the fruit mixture on top of the pastry and crimp the pastry edges. Bake in slow oven for 3-3½ hours.

Tipsy Laird

8 pieces of stale Swiss roll or stale cake
1 pint rich custard
½ pint double cream
¼ pint sherry
2 tbs. brandy
juice of 1 lemon and 1 orange
2 drops vanilla essence
raspberry jam

Cut up the Swiss Roll into eight equal pieces. Soak in the sherry. Pour the jam and the brandy (mixed together to thin the jam) over the Swiss roll. Leave to soak for about 5 minutes. Pour cooled custard over. Whip the cream and vanilla essence. Pile on top of the custard. Decorate with glace cherries and hazel nuts.

WELSH

Snowdon Pudding

8 oz. white breadcrumbs
8 oz. fine suet
5 large eggs
4 oz. stoned raisins
2 oz. cornflour
rind of 3 lemons
6 oz. brown (fine sugar)
5 oz. lemon marmalade
pinch of salt

Grease a large pudding basin well. Place some of the raisins on the base to decorate. Mix all the dry ingredients together. Beat the eggs and add to the mixture. Pour into the basin and tie securely with a cloth. Boil for 1½ - 1¾ hours.

Serve with wine sauce :

2 oz. sugar
1 teaspoon cornflour
rind of 1 lemon and juice
1½ oz. butter
1¾ glassful (6 oz. size) maderia or sweet sherry

Boil the wine and rind of the lemon and sugar till, the sugar has dissolved. Remove the rind. Melt the butter, and mix with the cornflour and wine. Add to the sugar mixture. Boil for one minute. Serve hot poured over the pudding.

Apple Cake

¾ cup sugar
4 oz. butter
2½ cups self raising flour
2 eggs
¾ cup of milk
1 lb stewed apples

Cream butter and sugar. Add eggs and beat. Fold in the flour and milk to make a soft dough. Roll out carefully. Cover a big plate with pastry. Spread stewed apples over and place the other half of the pastry on top. Bake in hot oven for 25 minutes. Eat hot or cold.
    Serves 8.

Monmouth Pudding

½ lb. white breadcrumbs
4 small eggs
4 tablespoons sugar (flavoured with 4 drops of vanilla essence)
¼ scant cup of hot milk
½ lb. strawberry jam
3 tablespoons melted butter
½ lb. chopped dried fruit
a little sherry

Pour the milk and sugar over the breadcrumbs. Leave to absorb the milk. Separate the yolks and whites of eggs. Whisk whites with half the sugar. Pour half the breadcrumb mixture into pudding dish — spread the base of the dish with the sherried soaked dried fruit (soak overnight for best results). Spread the jam over the breadcrumbs and finish off with the final amount of breadcrumb mixture.
Bake in a slow oven for 30 minutes or till set. Bring out and pour over whisked whites of eggs. Bake in very hot oven for 5 minutes until meringue is browned.

Rhubarb and Apple Crumble

1 lb. rhubarb
1 lb. apples
½ lb. self raising flour
4 oz. butter
4 oz. sugar
4 oz. porridge oats
4 oz. coconut
¼ oz. cinnamon
¼ oz. nutmeg

Clean and cook the fruit. Rub fat into flour. Add sugar and the other dry ingredients. Mix well. Place fruit in a large pie dish. Sprinkle crumble over the top. Bake in a moderate oven for 30 minutes. Serve hot with fresh cream or custard.

cakes

Cheese Cake

Approx. ½ lb. flaky pastry
1 lb. cream cheese
3 oz. sugar
3 eggs
1 oz. flour
pinch of cinnamon
pinch of salt
3 tablespoons melted butter
2 oz. grated plain dark chocolate

Cover the base and sides of a shallow dish with the rolled pastry. Separate the egg yolks and whites. Mix all the ingredients apart from the egg whites, together. Whisk the egg whites and add to the other mixture.

Fill case and cook in a hot oven. When cooked sprinkle with some sugar and a little more of the grated chocolate.

Vanilla Cake

2 lbs. plain flour
1½ lbs. butter
1 teaspoon vanilla essence
1 lb. sugar
2 eggs
½ lb. blanched almonds

Work all the ingredients to a firm dough. Make into small rounds and bake in a hot oven until brown.

Rum Tart

6 oz. rich short crust pastry
1 large cup fine breadcrumbs
juice of 1 lemon
pinch of salt
6 tablespoons black treacle

1 oz. rum
2 tablespoons coconut

Line a pie plate with the pastry and prick base. Mix other ingredients together. Fill the pastry case and bake in moderate to hot oven for about 20-25 minutes. Serve with cream.

Booty Cake

This cake could well have been made with the spoils of the smugglers that were around the Cornish Coves in the old times.

Soak
¼ lb. green cherries
½ lb. pineapple
½ lb. dessert dates
¼ lb. glace apricots
in
½ cup rum or brandy
Leave overnight if possible.

To the above add: ½ cup brown sugar creamed to 3 oz. butter, 2 beaten eggs and ½ cup plain flour, ½ teaspoon baking powder, 1 teaspoon vanilla essence and 1 teaspoon brandy. Pinch of salt.

Place in a greased cake tin and bake in moderate oven for approximately 1-1½ hours or until cooked. Leave for one whole day before cutting.

St. Ives Cake

1 lb. butter
1 lb. currants
2 lbs. flour
½ oz. yeast
½ lb. white sugar
2 oz. chopped peel
pinch salt
½ teaspoon saffron
½ teaspoon nutmeg
1¼ pints warm water

Mix yeast and some of the sugar to a cream. Rub the butter and flour to fine breadcrumb mixture. Add all other ingredients. Leave to rise in warm place to double in size. Punch down. Put into greased loaf or cake tins and let rise again. Bake in moderate oven for 1-1¼ hours.

Cool on rack.

Gingerbread Cake

¼ lb. butter
2 eggs
1 teacup milk
1 teaspoon mixed spice
½ cup currants
1 cup brown sugar
1 large tablespoon treacle
2 cups self-raising flour
½ teaspoon ginger
pinch salt

Cream butter and sugar. Add treacle. Add the eggs and milk, then fruit and flour. Bake in moderate oven for ¾ hour. Sprinkle the top with sugar.

IRISH

Apple and Potato Cake

¼ cup mashed cooked apple
¼ cup mashed cooked potatoes
1 teaspoon melted butter
1 cup sugar
1 well beaten egg
½ cup sultanas
¾ cup milk
2 drops lemon essence
2 cups self-raising flour
1 teaspoon nutmeg

Beat the butter into the apple and potato mixture.
Add the rest of the ingredients. Place in a greased cake tin. Sprinkle over the top the following topping:

1 cup plain flour
¼ cup melted butter
1 cup brown sugar
pinch cinnamon

Mix all well together. Bake in a moderate oven for 40 minutes. Leave to cool in the tin.

Whisky Cake

½ lb. self-raising flour
6 oz. butter
6 oz. brown sugar
2 tablespoons whisky
3 eggs
¼ lb. cherries (quartered)
1 teaspoon baking powder
pinch of salt
¼ lb. chopped almonds
(reserve a few for the top)

Soak the nuts in the whisky for about an hour.
Cream butter and sugar. Add the beaten eggs, nuts
and whisky, flour, baking powder and salt. Bake in
moderate oven for ¾ hour.

Lardy Cake

10 oz. lard
¾ lbs. brown sugar
2 lbs. warm risen bread dough
½ lb. currants

Flatten the dough to an oblong. Cut up lard to small
pieces. Place on top of dough. Sprinkle with the
sugar and currants. Bake in fairly hot oven for approx.
1-1¼ hours.

MANX

Soda Cakes

3 lbs. flour
¼ lb. lard
1 small teaspoon bicarbonade of soda
1 teaspoon salt
buttermilk

Mix the lard and flour to resemble fine breadcrumbs.
Add the salt, bicarbonate of soda and buttermilk to
form a soft dough. Roll out to ¼ inch thickness and
trim the edges to the shape required. Bake on a
griddle over a slow fire. Brown both sides.

Tynwald Cake

9 oz. butter
8 oz. flour
chocolate icing
1½ teaspoon ground ginger
few drops cochineal
1 oz. pistachio nuts
9 oz. castor sugar
6 eggs
3 oz. ground rice flour
1½ teaspoon baking powder
1½ teaspoon vanilla essence
cream filling

Line 3 round cake tins (8", 6", 4") with greased paper. Cream butter and sugar : add eggs one at a time. Add some flour with each egg. Mix flour, rice flour, ginger and baking powder. Stir lightly. Add essence and if needed, a little milk. Colour a delicate pink. Spread mixture over base of tins. Sprinkle tops with coconut and bake in moderate oven for ½ hour. When cold cover with chocolate icing. Place one cake on top of another, large at the base. Sprinkle with the chopped pistachio nuts. Place a small flag on top with the Manx coat of arms.

Cream filling :
4 oz. castor sugar
4 oz. unsalted butter
1 oz. glacé cherries
1 teaspoon vanilla essence

Cream sugar and butter. Add cherries and vanilla essence and mix.

Chocolate Icing :
½ lb. icing sugar
2-3 tablespoons hot water
small piece of lard
vanilla essence
2 oz. grated chocolate

Melt lard and chocolate. Mix in icing sugar. Add hot water. Add chocolate. Use at once.

Clootie Dumplings

1 lb. self-raising flour
¼ lb. suet
½ teaspoon salt
6 oz. sultanas
milk
½ teaspoon cinnamon
¼ lb. sugar
8 oz. currants
6 oz. raisins
½ teaspoon mixed spice
1 tablespoon treacle

Mix dry ingredients together. Stir in the treacle and enough milk to make a stiff dough. Place in a clean scalded cloth loosely (this pudding swells). Place in boiling water and cook for 3½-4 hours. Pull off cloth. Serve hot with custard as a pudding, or cold like a cake.

Dundee Cake

6 oz. flour
5 oz. butter
3 oz. currants
3 oz. cherries and raisins (mixed)
½ teaspoon baking powder
¼ teaspoon nutmeg
pinch of salt
6 oz. brown sugar
6 oz. sultanas
3 oz. mixed peel
¼ teaspoon mixed spice
3 beaten eggs
2 oz. almonds (for the top)

Cream the butter and sugar. Add the beaten eggs and flour. Add the fruit. Gradually add the spices, salt and baking powder. Place in a greased tin and put the almonds on the top in a circular shape. Bake in a moderate oven for 2½ hours or till middle is firm. Cool on tray and store for two days before cutting.

Scottish Beer Cake

1¾ cups brown sugar
1 cup softened butter
3 cups self-raising flour
4 eggs
1 cup chopped almonds
1 cup chopped walnuts
¾ cup beer
2 teaspoons baking powder

Cream butter and sugar. Add eggs and flour alternately. Add beer and then nuts. Decorate top of cake with a few of the nuts. Bake in a moderate oven for 1 hour.

Cool and leave for one day before eating.

Shortbread

12 oz. sugar
12 oz. plain flour
12 oz. ground rice
12 oz. butter
pinch of salt
2 eggs
2 tablespoons cream (single)

Rub the butter into all the dry ingredients. Beat the eggs and the cream together. Add to the mixture and knead until it is fine. Roll out to 1/8" thickness on a well greased board. Cut into fingers or bake in a mould. Prick with a fork before baking in a moderate oven until light gold colour. Cool.

WALES

Welsh Yeast Cake

1 lb. plain flour
¼ oz. yeast
½ lb. brown soft sugar
1 lb. sultanas, currants, mixed peel and a few cherries
(mixed)
½ lb. raisins
2 beaten eggs
pinch of salt
¼ teaspoon each of cinnamon, nutmeg and mixed spice
10 fluid oz. cold tea

Soak the fruit in the tea for about 4-6 hours. Mix the yeast and sugar to a cream, and add to the dry ingredients. Add the fruit and tea. Leave to prove for about three quarters of an hour in a warm place.

Bake in a slow to moderate oven for about 1-1½ hours.

This will make a good sized cake. Leave for one day before cutting.

64

Cacen Gneifio

2 eggs
½ lb. self-raising flour
½ lb. butter
½ lb. sugar
½ lb. currants
½ lb. sultanas
3 oz. almonds (slivered)
¼ lb. candied peel
½ cup sherry or port
pinch of salt
1½ teaspoons mixed spice

Cream the sugar and butter. Add the eggs to the mixture with a little flour to stop the mixture from curdling. Sift the flour and salt. Add the nuts and fruit to the sifted flour and stir well into the mixture. Place into a greased baking tin and bake for approximately 1-2 hours in a moderate oven. Before baking sprinkle the top with nuts.

Cage Bach

1 lb. self-raising flour
10 oz. butter
6 oz. sugar
8 oz. mixed fruit
2 eggs
pinch of salt
3 tablespoons milk

Sift the salt and flour. Rub in the butter till it resembles fine breadcrumbs. Beat the eggs and milk and add to the dry mixture to make a stiff dough. Roll out onto a floured board. Cut into small rounds. Cook on a griddle for about 3 minutes.

This mixture will make about three dozen cakes, which will keep for about a fortnight in an airtight tin.

Teisen Lap *(Plate Cake)*

1 lb. self-raising flour
½ lb. butter
pinch of nutmeg
¼ lb. sugar
2 eggs
½ pint buttermilk
½ lb. mixed fruit (currants, sultanas, raisins)

Rub the butter into the flour. Add the other dry ingredients. Beat the eggs well and add to the milk. Add the liquid to the dry mixture to make a soft dough. Grease a shallow dish and bake in a moderate oven for about half an hour.

These cakes are made and eaten all over Wales. Teisen means 'tart' or 'cake' — Lap, a 'plate'.

Teisen Galan Gaeaf

¾ lb. plain flour
pinch of salt
1 teaspoon baking powder
½ lb. butter
½ lb. sugar
4 eggs
1¼ lbs. mixed fruit (1 lb. fruit — ¼ lb. nuts,
blanched almonds and walnuts)

Cream butter and sugar. Add eggs, one at a time, and beat till fluffy. Add the sifted flour and salt. Fold in, and lastly, fold in the fruit and nuts. Bake in a lined and greased cake tin in a slow to moderate oven for about two hours. This cake may be iced if desired.

Huish Cake

8 oz. butter
8 oz. flour
1 lb. castor sugar
8 eggs
8 oz. ground rice
caraway seeds

Cream butter and sugar. Separate eggs. Beat yolks into butter and sugar mixture. Add flour and rice.

Whisk egg whites until stiff. Add to the mixture and stir well with a steel spoon. Add caraway seeds. Grease two 7" tins and bake in moderate oven for 1¼ hours.

This cake was served at a baby's christening ceremony, or sometimes for "high tea" on Sundays.

Tarten Llysiau Duon Bach

8 oz. short crust pastry

Prepare the pastry and line a shallow baking tin with it. Prick the base and blind bake for 20 minutes.

1 lb. berries
¼ lb. sugar
½ cup water
1½ tsp. gelatine
½ pint fresh cream

Clean and wash the berries and cook till soft. Cool. Add the sugar and dissolve the gelatine in the water. Pour gelatine over fruit and pour into pastry case. Whip cream and decorate the top of the tart with the cream.

Llysiau Duon Bach are very like Bilberries and as children we used to eat them from the hedges on our way home from school in the summer.

drinks

Punch

1 bottle rum
1 bottle brandy
4 oz. sugar
juice of 6 lemons
pinch of nutmeg, cinnamon and cloves
2½ bottles iced water or soda water

Place the spices and sugar with the water in a pan.
Boil for 5 minutes. Strain when cold, add rum and
brandy.

Ginger Beer

juice of 2 lemons
1 gallon water
1 oz. ginger
1 lb. sugar
½ oz. yeast
2 oz. cream of tartar

Place water in a large saucepan : add the lemon juice,
sugar and cream of tartar. Bring to the boil and leave
to get luke warm. When still luke warm add the yeast
and leave in a warm place for 24 hours. Strain and
bottle. Use in about four days.

Irish Coffee

Heat an Irish coffee tankard. Pour one jigger of Irish whisky into the tankard. Add 3 cubes of sugar and top with black coffee to within an inch of the top. Stir to dissolve coffee. Add whipped cream. Do not stir after cream has been added.

This recipe was given to me by a Dublin lass and this little ditty came with it :

Coffee rich as an Irish brogue
Coffee strong as friendly hands,
Sugar sweet as a tongue of a rogue
Whisky smooth as the wit of the bard.

The Toast — Slainte   (Good Health)

Punch

Combine in a large punch bowl, 2 quarts sweet cider, half bottle vodka, ¼ bottle Irish whisky and ¼ bottle sweet sherry. Slice 3 oranges and 2 lemons, and add these together with 2 oz. sugar. Chop some mint, add and chill. Lastly add a syphon of soda and ice cubes. Makes about 20 helpings.

Beetroot Wine

    1 oz. fresh yeast
    2 oranges (juice and peel)
    4 lbs sugar
    2 oz. lime juice
    2 lemons (juice and peel)
    4-5 quarts water
    6 lbs old beetroot

Cook the beetroot in water. When cooked, peel and chop up into small pieces. Pour the water into a large stew pan and add the beetroot, sugar, and the juices and peels of the citrus fruits. Add the lime juice. Bring slowly to the boil and boil for about 5-10 mins. Cool to lukewarm and add the yeast. Allow to ferment in an earthenware jar or crock for at least a week. Stir well each day. Strain, bottle and keep in a dark place for at least six months — longer if possible.

Potato Wine

    ½ pound potatoes
    3 pieces ginger
    2 lemons
    1 gallon cold water
    3½ lbs sugar
    2 oranges

Place the peeled and cut potatoes, ginger and water into a large pan. Boil for 15 minutes. When cool, strain the potato water onto the juices of the lemons, oranges and sugar. Boil for another ¾ hour very slowly. Allow to get cold. When quite cold bottle in clean bottles and when the wine has stopped fermenting cork well. Keep in a dark place for 3-4 months.

Hot Toddy

¼ cup boiling water
¼ cup whisky
2 tablespoons honey
¼ teaspoon lemon juice

Melt the honey in the boiling water. Add the lemon juice and whisky. Drink whilst hot.

A toddy was traditionally stirred with a silver spoon and served in a crystal glass. An earthenware mug does not, however, crack so easily.

Athol Brose

1¼ pints whiskey
1 lb. honey
1 cup cold water

Place honey in a large pan. Add water. Heat until honey is dissolved. Add whiskey when cooled. Stir until it becomes frothy. Bottle and cork.

Rowanberry Liqueur

1 cup rowanberries
1 pint Brandy
syrup
(1 pint cold water and 2 lbs sugar)

Leave the berries on a shelf until dried and shrivelled. Place the berries in the brandy and leave for at least a week. Strain and mix with the syrup. Bottle and cork.

The berries are picked around September and the Liqueur should not be drunk before Christmas time.

Medd *(Mead)*

4 pints honey
2 gallons water
4 lemons
1 oz. cloves
2 lbs. white sugar
piece of ginger (scoured)
2 oz. yeast
small piece of bread

Spread the yeast on a piece of bread. Boil the water honey and sugar. Stand in an earthenware pot. Skim off any scum. Add lemon juice, cloves and ginger. Leave to cool. When just warm float the bread and yeast on the top. Cover with a clean cloth. Leave for about 6-8 days. Strain and bottle. Corks should be loose to start with. Leave for at least 5-6 months.

Diod Fain

There are numerous ways of making this Welsh wine, but this is just one recipe :

2 lbs. white sugar
2 gallons water
4 large lemons
2 oz. fresh yeast
3 oz. stem root ginger

Squeeze the lemons and grate a little of the peel away. Pour the juice over the sugar. Bruise the ginger and place all the ingredients in a pan. Pour over the boiling water and leave to cool. When nearly cold add the yeast and leave to stand for a whole day. Bottle between 24 — 36 hours. Leave for 1 week — then it is ready to drink.

OTHERS

Cheese Soufflé

6 eggs
1 tablespoon breadcrumbs
1½ oz. butter
1 oz. flour
cayenne pepper
salt and pepper
¾ pint milk
teaspoon mustard
3 oz. grated cheese

Grease and prepare the soufflé dish. Melt the butter: add flour and the salt and pepper. Add milk and whisk to a smooth paste. When slightly cooled add the mustard, cheese, cayenne pepper and egg yolks. In a large bowl whisk egg whites until stiff. Fold into the sauce mixture and bake in hot oven for ½ hour. Serve immediately.

Lemon Butter

1 lb. butter
2½ cups castor sugar
1 cup lemon juice
8 eggs (well beaten)

Place all ingredients in a double boiler. Cook for approximately 20 minutes.

Use for sandwich cake fillings and tartlets. Keeps well.

Creme Brulee

¾ pint single cream
1 pint double cream
3 tablespoons castor sugar
6 small egg yolks
5 tablespoons brown sugar

Heat the cream and sugar in a double boiler for 2 minutes. Remove from the heat. Add egg yolks. Stir well. Cook for 5 more minutes. Pour cream brulee into a wetted mould and chill for at least 6 hours. Just before serving, sprinkle brown sugar over top and grill until melted.

Mayonnaise

3 egg yolks
½ teaspoon lemon juice
pinch of black pepper
¾ pint olive oil
½ teaspoon vinegar
½ teaspoon salt

Whip the egg yolks. Add lemon juice, vinegar and salt. Add oil, drop by drop and beat well. Add pepper. Keep in an airtight container.

IRISH

Baked Potatoes

Wash and scrub the potatoes and place amongst the hot ashes under the fire. Leave until soft. Split in half and eat with butter and black pepper.

Redcurrant Jelly

1¼ lbs. sugar
6 lbs redcurrants

Wash and clean the currants. Place into a large pan and add just enough water to cover the base of the pan. Simmer gently for about ¾ - 1 hour. When cooked, leave to strain through a muslin bag. Measure the juice and add 1¼ lb. sugar to each pint of juice. Bring to the boil for 2 minutes. Cool slightly and bottle into warmed jars.

Porridge

    4 oz. oatmeal
    1¼ pints cold water
    pinch of salt

In Scotland the porridge is always stirred with a spurtle.

    I do not know if the porridge tasted better when the spurtle was used but I was told by an old Scottish friend that porridge not stirred with a spurtle is not porridge!

Tablet

    1 lb. sugar
    1 gill water
    1 tablespoon glucose sugar
    ¼ lb. butter
    ½ teaspoon vinegar
    2 oz. almonds

Put the sugar and glucose into the water and heat until dissolved. Boil gently for ten minutes. Add the butter and vinegar. Cook until it will set when a drop is placed in cold water. Add the almonds just before taking off the heat.

Stovies

    2 oz. dripping
    salt and pepper
    1 small onion
    about 1 lb. potatoes
    left over cold meat
    approx ¼ - ½ pint water or stock

Cut the potatoes into cubes. Place meat, diced onion and potatoes in a pan. Season. Cover and cook for 10-15 minutes on a low heat. Serve with fresh parsley sprinkled over the top.

    This is one way the Scots have of using up cold meat. It's a good supper dish on a cold winter's night.

Tymplen Ceirch *(Dumplings)*

1 lb. fine oatmeal
4 oz. butter
6 oz. self raising flour
4 oz. currants
pinch of salt
1½ cups of buttermilk

Mix dry ingredients together. Add enough milk to make into a fine dough. Roll into small balls in floured hands. Cook very gently in boiling water for about 40-50 minutes. Drain and serve hot.

These dumplings are a very old and traditional dish of Wales and can be served with cawl, ham, or as a sweet pudding with warm custard.

Bara Lawr *(Laverbread)*

1 lb. prepared laver bread
2 oz. butter
little lemon juice
2 oz. oatmeal

The seaweed needs to be boiled for six hours or so, or until it is soft. When soft, cut into servable pieces and coat with the oatmeal. Fry the pieces in the hot butter for about 5-10 minutes. Eat hot. Sprinkle with a little lemon juice.

Laver bread is sold in the fish markets of Wales and it should be eaten as fresh as possible. It is therefore not a good idea to buy laverbread in bulk!

Cyflaith

½ lb. brown sugar
6 oz. golden syrup
6 oz. butter
few drops of vinegar

Place all ingredients into a large saucepan and boil together for about ten minutes, or until the mixture forms a soft ball when a drop is placed in cold water. When ready pour into a greased flat tin. Cut into squares when cool and store in an airtight tin.

This was often made for the "calennig children" who called to wish the family a Happy New Year on the first day of the year.

Shincyn

½ pint milk
1 slice thick buttered toast
1 tablespoon sugar
drop of tea

Boil the milk. Cut bread into cubes. Add sugar and a little tea — just to add colour. Pour over milk.

This was a supper dish in West Wales but how it got the name "Shincyn" has remained a mystery.

Welsh Rarebit

4 slices of toast
½ lb. sharp cheese (grated)
4 tablespoon brown ale
2 oz. butter
salt and pepper
pinch of mustard

Put the ale into a saucepan and add the cheese. Melt very slowly. Add the seasonings and butter. Toast and butter the bread. When mixture is very hot pour over the toast and grill until browned. Serve at once.

•

ENWAU CYMRAEG I BLANT /WELSH NAMES FOR CHILDREN 65c
Ruth Stephens
A comprehensive collection of over 800 Welsh personal names, with translations and explanations. Ideal for impending parents!

CORNISH IS FUN 75c
Richard Gendall & Tim Saunders
A new, popular course in living Cornish, on the lines of 'Welsh is Fun'. Distributed in Cornwall by Lodenek Press, 14/16 Market St., Padstow (Tel. 283).

WELSH IS FUN-TASTIC! 85p
Heini Gruffudd & Elwyn Ioan
The follow-up to 'Welsh is Fun' but funnier (bluer?) still. Includes revision lessons. New redesigned paperback edition.

THE RISE OF THE WELSH REPUBLIC 90c
Derrick Hearne
A "model" of life in the first ten years of a sovereign Welsh Republic established in the near future, in the Age of Scarcity. A serious, ambitious work covering government, economics, education and defence.

THE JOY OF FREEDOM £1.85
Derrick Hearne
A collection of wide-ranging essays attempting to lay the basis for "An Ideology of Welsh Liberation" strong enough to challenge English imperialism and its manipulation of the media.